He Watched and Took Note

Curtis Becker

 Press

Emporia, KS

He Watched and Took Note
Copyright © 2018 Curtis Becker

All rights reserved. No part of this publication may be reproduced, distributed, or transmitted in any form or by any means, without prior written permission of the publisher.

This is a work of fiction. The names, characters, places, and incidents are either a product of the author's imagination or used fictitiously, and any resemblance to actual persons living or dead, business establishments, events, or locals is entirely coincidental.

Published by Kellogg Press
1114 Commercial St.
Emporia, Kansas 66801
kelloggpress.com

Hazel Hart, Editor
hazelhart.com

Dave Leiker, Cover and Author Photos
daveleikerphotography.com

Austin Anderson, The Watcher

Kari Ludes, Interior Art
kludes@g.emporia.edu

Joe & Rita Buchanan, Proofreading

Curtis Becker, Project Manager/Layout and Design
curtis@curtisbeckerbooks.com

ISBN: 978-0-692-15677-3

Library of Congress Control Number: 2018908884

Dedication

This book is dedicated to my parents, Gordon and Toni. My happy childhood was a product of their hard work and sacrifices. My days were full of reading, creating, imagining, and playing. I will never forget the example they provided of how one makes this world a better place and would not be who I am today if not for them. This book's release date, August 17, 2018, would have been my dad's 70th birthday. Happy Birthday!

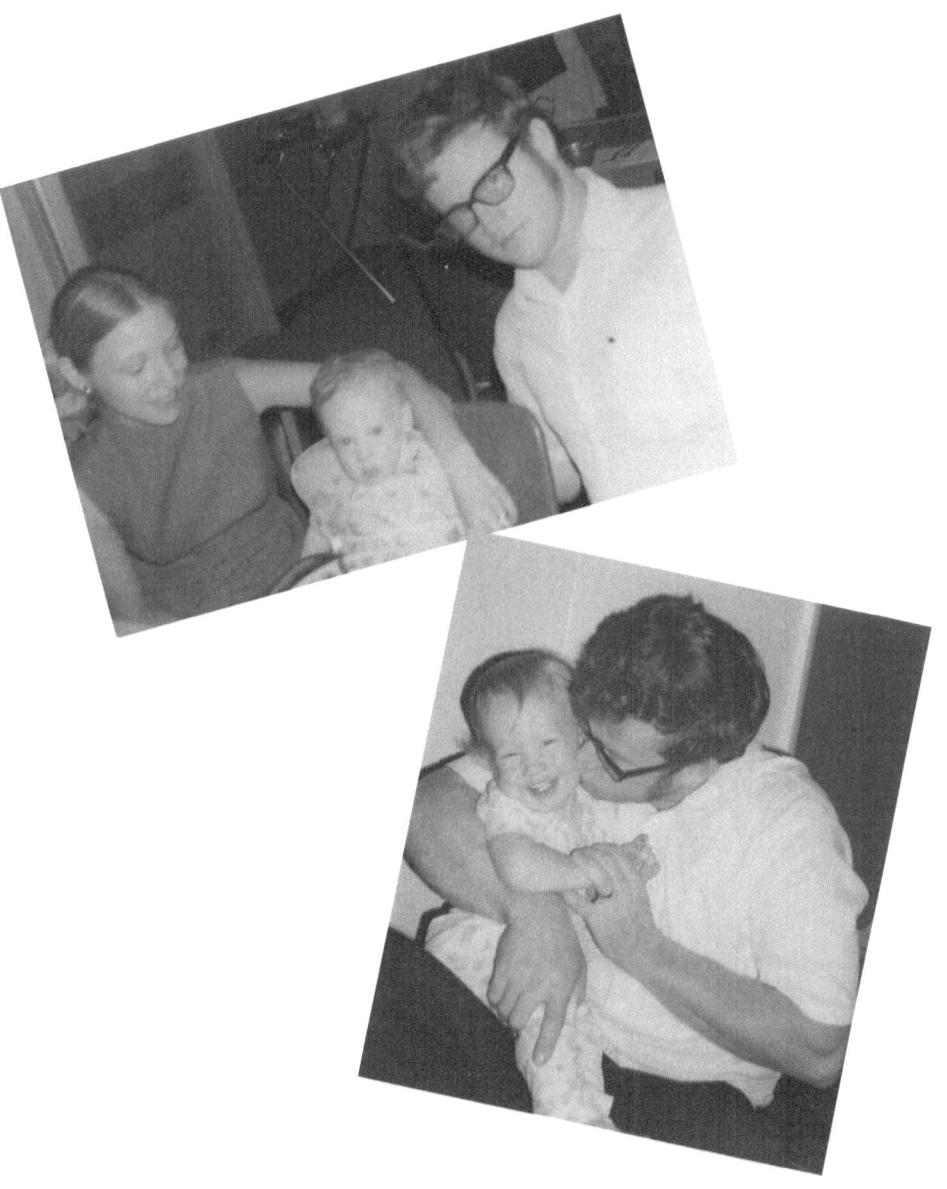

Table of Contents

My Childhood Teddy Bear	1
You Won't Give Up	5
I Saw the Light	9
My New Job	11
What's a Matter with Kansas, Now?	15
The Nutritional Value of Stale Cheese Balls	17
The Sage of Emporia, 2018	21
He Watched and Took Note	23
the poet	27
A Modern Hero	29
A Real Love Poem	33
Smothered by Words	35
The Overlord of Ice and Snow	37
The Domain of Bob's Sack 'N Save	41
The Relationship Cycle	43
It's Time	45
the process i can't control	49

Forgiveness	51
Modern Sonnet #13	55
The Starlight Motor Lodge	57
I'm Not Kevin Rabas	63
Frank Won't Back Down	65
Writing Love Poems with Kevin	67

Life is deep and simple,
and what our society gives us is shallow and complicated.

Mister Fred Rogers

My Childhood Teddy Bear

My childhood teddy bear
now sits in a rocking chair
unassuming, his look austere
I feel bad about his matted hair

"Is it love if it hurts you?"
I wonder aloud
He is stoic in his refusal to respond

Some of my friends ask "why"
Why do you keep that old bear?
That one with a missing clump of hair
The one resting upon the rocking chair

Loyalty?
Friendship?
Insecurity?
Innocence lost?

I used to care
that you might find out about my bear
that old austere lump of hair
slouching in that old rocking chair

That bear has a tattoo
of grape jelly
on his left ass cheek

That missing eye
makes him look B. A.
I should have found him the pirate patch

Mr. Bear?
Did Mike Tyson get ahold of your ear?
Stoic!

Curtis Becker

The survivor of my love
slumps over the rail
of my rocking chair

I do not see his pain.

My five-year-old eyes see a bear
in good repair
with nary a tear
and all of his hair
There's no despair!

Thank you, Grandma, for giving me my teddy bear!

"My Childhood Teddy Bear" originally appeared in B*ards Against Hunger: 5th Anniversary Edition.*

He Watched and Took Note

You Won't Give Up
Dust Bowl on the High Plains

The hot wind bites your face as you cover it to protect it from the dust. Your other hand grasps your lifeline, the rope strung from the barn to the house. Your hands, calloused by hard work and harder conditions, don't feel the fibers poke into skin as you feel your way in the blinding storm. Entering the house, you slam the door on the tormenting winds outside. This doesn't stop them or even quiet them. They howl as they circle and whip around the tiny structure you call a home. A quick inspection of the windows shows that the sheets your wife installed and sealed with a homemade paste are holding. She did this shortly before she left for her parents' house in Iowa. The lone chair in the center of the room is the most basic of chairs but provides comfort to your weary body. You drop yourself onto it. The only other furniture in the room is a table in the corner. On it rests the only picture in the house; it is a family portrait. You are smiling and look robust in the picture; your hand is on your beautiful wife's shoulder. You feel you would forget what she looks like if not for this reminder. Your children, two boys and a little girl, are grouped around and in front of their mother. You miss them desperately, but with little Suzie's Dust Lung, back east with the in-laws was the perfect place for your family. You won't give up. Your duty is to save this farm. How?

The minutes seem like hours; you look at your pocket watch, a gift from your father. Hopefully, this duster will stop soon. There is a social at the church this evening. Just a skeleton group is left from the original congregation, but you aren't complaining about the less than fancy nature of the socials now-a-days. Being social is about the only element left from the good times. Nobody brings food anymore, and there are very few families left. Many people have just abandoned their land and headed to California or back east. You are determined to stay put. You won't give up. You can't give up. You hope the "social" will happen; this is your only opportunity to see other people in quite some time. You miss conversation, and find that you talk to yourself sometimes or the animals, what's left of them. It's not that you are crazy or anything; you are just exercising your vocal cords.

The pocket watch tells you that you missed the church "social." Not that anyone else would have made it. The good reverend could have managed to come from the parsonage, but he wouldn't have tried. He would have known nobody else would make it. The fact that you missed out on this event is really a blow to your spirits. You need to talk to other people.

The sky gets even darker as somewhere beyond the monster cloud of dust the sun sets. You sit in the dark—no need to waste a candle—and listen to the dust sandblast the side of the house. The wind howls. You begin to think it might be communicating. If you could just understand its song, maybe you could make it go away. You listen intently as it rages and bellows. You follow the crescendos of the wail; you listen to the eerie melody mesmerize you. You can't give up. Hold on. The black of night engulfs you as your mind finds an uneasy sleep.

You awaken. The song has ended. Bright sunlight fills the room. You push the door open and make your way outside to survey the damage. A blizzard of sand-like dirt has blown and drifted in your yard. You grab the scoop shovel and clear the doorway and steps. You begin to work your way to the barn; you follow the rope, this time with your eyes. You are careful not to touch metal objects, including your truck. You know that dust storms can electrify these objects and send a grown man to the ground. You used to like to watch the static electricity arc in the blades in the windmill. This was before the storms got so regular and so intense. You think back to last night and your brush with madness. How much longer can you take living in this forsaken place? Granted, it wasn't always a forsaken place. It was once a hearty land. Throwing seeds at the rich dirt basically guaranteed a bumper crop. Those were the good years.

What happened? Did this community do something to offend God? Why would He let all of you suffer like this? Your worst fears are confirmed when you reach the barn. What was left of the animals, a malnourished cow and an old goat, didn't survive. Their lifeless shells were haphazardly deposited on the ground. In your haste to get to the house, you didn't secure the door, and they wandered out into the storm. Their lungs were no doubt filled with dirt. Dusty paste matted in their eyes and fine silt clung to their hides. The remains would have been hard to look at, but these poor creatures were so malformed in life and in death that the corpses seem surreal and grotesque, not sickening. Suffering for your animals has come to an end. You drop the shovel and go back to the house. Sitting back down on the chair, you realize that you are now truly alone. You can't give up. You won't give up. It is always darkest before the dawn.

You contemplate butchering the animals for what little meat is on their bones, but, you have learned to ignore the pain of hunger and are a little too tired to deal with it, a little too tired to deal with any of it right now. Your mind begins to wander. You think of all the people you have known and loved in your life. You think of your excitement when you brought your family out to the high plains of Western Kansas. You think of how you bragged to your extended family about how you were going to make it big as a farmer and landowner. Nobody would want to own this land now. Don't give up! You walk out to your truck and gingerly touch the handle. No shock. You open the door and clean the dirt out as best you can. You go back into the house and gather the chair, the table, and the picture. They are placed in your truck; a pile of your clothes is in the passenger seat. At least you have company. Where are you going? You aren't giving up? It's really green in Iowa this time of year.

I Saw the Light

I saw the light.

I saw the light and I knew.

I saw the light and I knew where I was going.

I saw the light and I knew that I was going on the right path.

I saw the light on the right path, and I knew my actions were justified. I stood with my head tall.

I stood with my head tall, because I knew I was on the right path.

I stood with my head tall, because I knew.

I stood tall; I saw the light.

I stood in the light.

My New Job

My best friend Patrick and I left Kansas City on Friday. The Impala handled really well for an older car; I didn't mind being behind the wheel. By the time we got west of Dallas, I needed to stop. My butt was a little sweaty, and the car was getting stuffy. The AC was trying to keep up, but this was west Texas in July. We had been driving down the highway for quite some time. The thick trees and tall grass surrounding the road all day had given way to lone trunks with sparse branches standing sentinel over strips of brown vegetation. This scenery was not on any post cards. Perhaps, someone at sometime had tried to capture the stark beauty of this land and sell it to the masses; however, that person would have lost his or her proverbial shirt. I wouldn't have purchased one, and I grew up here. These scenes and the lonely roads that cut through the landscape were all too familiar to me, but would have been something new to Patrick. He was currently sleeping in the passenger seat, so I kept on driving. I thought back to the last time I had seen these roads five years ago; they hadn't really changed at all, save the weathering of the billboards. I smiled as my friend slept; Patrick coming with me gave me the strength to make this trip. Technically, I guess I came with him because the Impala was his car. But, this was my trip. I was just lucky to have a best friend who was willing to do this with me or for me.

When we finally got out of the car, Grandpa was sitting in his undershirt on an old metal chair on the edge of his weathered porch. The old man seemed happy to see me, but he was working hard to muffle his joy and excitement. I had been up this driveway a million times and had walked up the sidewalk to the house a million more. This time was different. Grandpa planted his hands on the arms of the chair and struggled to get up; however, I hugged him before he could stand. He really smelled like "old man" now. Patrick and Grandpa became fast friends as I went into the house to find something cold to drink. It was the same house, but in some way it wasn't. The knick-knacks and decorations were still there. Even the clown statue stood in its customary spot by the fireplace. When I was just as tall as it, the seemingly happy clown haunted my dreams. Today it seemed innocent. I went into the kitchen, and for the first time, my nose did not alert me to something wonderful in the oven. The kitchen that had always been warm and inviting now seemed cold, sterile, and sad. There was no tea in the ice box. I found some cans of pop and brought three of them out to the porch. It was good to be with Grandpa.

The old man was up at dawn the next morning and woke me up with the sound of his making coffee. He never had been quiet in the morning. I skillfully descended from the top bunk of my old bunk bed, careful not to wake Patrick in the bottom one. My bare feet swum through the thick shag carpet; the sensation transported me back fifteen years. I felt like a kid again; it reminded me of the first time my feet were buried in this carpet. Grandpa had just brought me home the night before, and after falling out of the bunk bed, I had luxuriated in the experience of the carpet on my skin. It was so warm and safe. In an instant the present returned, and Grandpa was pouring me a cup of coffee. We sat at the table. It was much like that first morning so many years ago. We tried to make small talk, but the words were awkward and uncomfortable. Back then, Grandma had turned her attention from the breakfast feast she was preparing on the stove to interject her calm easy nature into the conversation. Today she wasn't there. The stove was cold and lifeless. Grandpa sipped his coffee. I told him I was sorry as I put my hand on his. He told me that he knew and asked what Patrick and I wanted for breakfast.

The breakfast at The Pancake House was okay. It wasn't like Grandma would have made, but we were glad to have it. Patrick was the spark our conversation needed. He asked Grandpa lots of questions and Grandpa regaled him with many stories. I knew all of the stories; they were mostly about me. Grandpa got that misty twinkle in his eye as he recounted my first day at a new school, my little league games, my first love, my first job, my first car, my first car wreck. He enjoyed the trip down memory lane. Patrick enjoyed finding out more about his best friend. I enjoyed knowing that Grandpa remembered all of these things about me.

Before heading back to Grandpa's house, we went to the cemetery. I brought an assortment of plastic flowers to leave with Grandma. Actually, Patrick brought them. This was my trip, but he had organized it and then forced me to go. We helped Grandpa to her grave. The dirt was fresh and a temporary marker stood in the spot where the stone would be placed when the monument company was finished making it. I wished I could be there alone. I didn't want Patrick to see me cry; I didn't want Grandpa to see me cry. Since the phone call a month ago, my countenance was stoic and measured. No emotion. No crying. Today it all came out in the form of an ugly cry. My sobbing, shaking self was helped to the car by Patrick and Grandpa. Grandpa's steady hand on my arm made everything okay, just like it always had. That day was a bit of a turning point for me; I knew I couldn't leave my grandpa all alone here.

    We stayed with Grandpa for several more days, helping him get caught up on chores and fixing things around the house. I mowed the lawn. It was that same mower that Grandpa bought when I turned twelve. Back then, he had told me that it was my new mower and my new "job" was to keep the grass nice and tidy. I found that I was still able to expertly maneuver around the obstacles in the yard, even though it had been years since I practiced. On the evening before we were to leave, Grandpa was working up the courage to ask me something. When he finally did ask, it was the one thing I was hoping he wouldn't ask. He wanted help going through grandma's things. The bedrooms were small in this old house, and Grandma had always kept the third bedroom as her room. It was the place she kept all of her things. She dressed in that room and "put on her face" there. When we opened the door, I could smell her perfume hanging in the air. Grandpa sat in the large overstuffed chair at her makeup table and Patrick sat cross-legged on the floor as I began opening drawers and doors. We laughed and cried as we boxed up a lifetime of memories. Many of the items would be going to my aunts. The photo albums would be staying with Grandpa. Each picture we encountered was expertly labeled with grandma's tight neat cursive. Grandpa tried to give me some, but I declined. I told him that they could stay with him, and I would just have to visit Texas more often.

    Now that I am back in Kansas City, I realize that I am not going to be able to keep my promise to Grandpa. I won't be visiting more often. I am moving home. Yes, home. My life here, will be missed, but I belong with Grandpa. When I was all alone in the world, he and grandma were there for me. It is my turn to be there for him. Life takes unexpected twists and turns, and I am happy about this one.

Curtis Becker

What's a Matter with Kansas, Now?

What's the matter with Kansas?
Now

Do we have any
money
in this state?
Money for kids?
Money for pot holes?

They say follow the trail
Is there even enough money
for a trail?

what about the Arts?
Are they important?

Poetry
Theatre
Journalism
Painting
Sculpture
Philosophy

Important?
Funded?

Maybe, if we stop thinking,
nothing will seem a matter
with Kansas
anymore

Written as a tribute to William Allen White on the occasion of his 150th birthday.

The Nutritional Value of Stale Cheese Balls

The year was 2033, and order had finally been restored. Things had been quite out of hand thanks to greedy and corrupt politicians and the people who kept voting them into office. The momentum of voting a fool from one party into office as retribution for the previous fool from another party became a bit counterproductive. Citizens were engaged in vicious meme wars on social media that threatened to undermine the productivity of society. Corrupt politicians stoked the fire with one hand and pocketed obscene amounts of money with the other. Luckily, The American Bureaucratic Committee for Decency, Ethics, and Fairness established guidelines for behavior and discourse after its creation prior to the election of 2032.

This year, the rules dictated that a Purple Party candidate must be procured from sector 27G, Mr. Preston Christianson received a knock at his door. Mr. Christianson had not chosen the Purple Party after conducting extensive research on the party platform. He rather liked the color purple and found the scent of lavender to be almost intoxicating. Each month, he copied, from the ABCDEF repository, his obligatory social media posts extolling the virtues of his party; however, his party's platform was somewhat ambiguous.

When the loud, sharp knock came from the other side of his door on that hot and sticky July morning, Mr. Christianson was finishing his posts. The ABCDEF G-Men on the other side of the door wasted little time in quizzing him on his political beliefs. He was woefully ill prepared! Christianson reached into the dark and dusty recesses of his mind but came up with nothing but a few platitudes and a hashtag that was popular two years ago. Luckily, the two sharp-dressed men on Mr. Christianson's stoop were able to provide a laminated sheet. It was colored purple to avoid confusion.

Christianson rather enjoyed his current position as a social media compliance officer and was sad that he was going to have to run for Congress; however, it was his civic duty to participate in the process. He loved spending hours online, checking members for appropriate posts, memes, and hashtags. Now, that part of his life was over. Christianson began to memorize the speech that one of the ABCDEF G-Men had handed him while the other fitted him with his corporate donor suit. All of the corporations that had bought and paid for Mr. Christianson would be represented by patches sewn onto his suit. The bigger the patch, the larger the 'donation.'

Curtis Becker

This was a fabulous way to keep the voters informed. Unfortunately, most voters still didn't follow the money. If you were a Purple Party Patriot, you voted Purple Party no matter what.

Across town, Mr. Adams was being fitted for his suit. The recesses of his mind were darker and dustier than those of Mr. Christianson. Adams, the candidate of the Orange Party Optimists, beamed with pride and ushered a handful of cheese balls past his three chins and into his waiting mouth.

"You must eat the whole handful," his friends always said.

On the morning of the first debate, it was Christianson versus Adams pairing off in the double elimination round of the 2033 Election Bracket. Each man delivered a series of scripted sound bites that were lapped up by the media. The pro-Purple media anointed Christianson the savior of the country and extolled his many virtues while bemoaning the very existence of a man like Adams. It was almost a certainty that his getting this close to government would be the ruination of the country, the system, and the souls of everyone and anyone. The pro-Orange media saw things a bit differently.

As the debate dragged on, Adams began to shovel cheese balls into his mouth. Orange dust clung to two of the three chins, his tie, and his lapels. He was talking about family values. His voice droned on. His opponent Christianson was distracted, even mesmerized by the fluid motion. Adams's chubby hands secured a large quantity of cheese balls from the podium. Values! With a scooping action the paws avoided the flapping of chin one. Values! Chin two! Values! Chin three! He couldn't think. Laminated purple swam before his eyes. Words crashed into one another.

At that moment something happened. Something that would change the course of history. Rather than succumb to the situation, Christianson, the man from Sector 27 G, the man who found lavender intoxicating, the man who just wanted to be a low-level cog in the government machine, had an original thought. More than that, he allowed it to pass his lips. It flew to the microphone and reverberated around the world. The ABCDEF G-Men didn't know what to do when someone went off script. The media outlets didn't know what to do; the sponsors didn't know what to do; the people didn't know what to do. The utterance became known as the phrase that echoed around the world. It was so brilliant in its simplicity while its complexity became fodder for future books and intellectual debates.

Christianson went on to win. All he had done that day was forget to censor what he said, and the question in his mind escaped.

"What is the nutritional value of stale cheese balls?"

The Sage of Emporia, 2018

on Commercial Street
at the China Dragon

You will make a change for the better
within the year;
The great aim of education is not knowledge
but action;

A great pleasure in life is doing
what others say you can't;
Big things coming in future—
only matter of time;

Lucky numbers
3,7,10,18

mixed with rice,
bamboo shoots,
and egg drop soup.

Written as a tribute to William Allen White on the occasion of his 150th birthday.

Curtis Becker

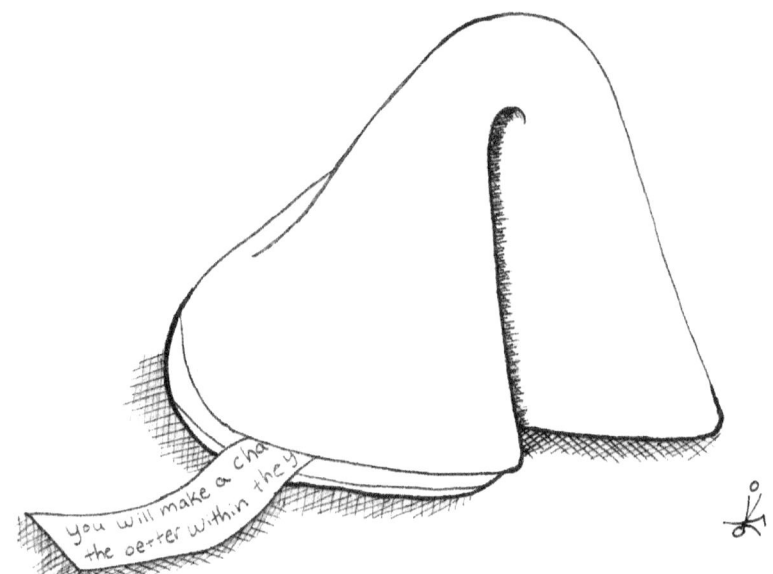

He Watched and Took Note

15:19
The boy was happy as he left the large office building and a meeting with Mr. Franklin. The transaction was complete. He now had enough money to get more baccen powder to stick up his nose. His body could taste the pleasure it brought, and the thought of it hastened his steps. He touched his pocket and felt the small bulge from something concealed inside, his insurance. The boy scampered down the street from awning to canopy, trying to avoid the heat of the afternoon sun or someone watching from above. His erratic pattern may have seemed comical to anyone else observing, but not to the one watching from a nearby roof. The observer knew that this child was a loose end that must be dealt with. A poisoned dart fired from a mechanism mounted on his wrist did the deed. As the boy died, the man on the roof watched and took note.

15:01
Franklin admired the medallion in his hands. He studied it; he smiled at its beauty. He got lost in a daydream but was brought crashing back to reality as the com panel on his desk sounded a high-pitched, urgent wail. Franklin pressed the large button on its face, and an image of his assistant was standing in miniature on his massive oak desk. She informed him that he had an urgent visitor. The boy was not dead yet but would be soon; the transaction was not complete. The hair on Franklin's neck stood up. He hurriedly slipped the medallion into the pocket of his suit jacket and stood up as his assistant ushered the green clad lad into his steel and plastic office. Its mute colors and efficient design stood in sharp contrast to the large desk, a keepsake that he lugged to each office he occupied. It suited Franklin, as he was a large man.

With a swagger, the boy walked in, threw himself in a chair, and put his bare feet on the corner of the desk. The skinny legs barely reached because of his incredibly short stature. The soles of his soiled feet were black from the grime of the street. Franklin was not happy but bit his tongue.

"It is done," was all the boy said as he cocked his head and smiled a greedy, little smile.

Franklin removed several gold coins from a pouch on his waist. He threw them at the boy who retrieved them from the desk top. The weird child patted the man on the back and gave him a sideways "bro" hug. The large man jerked away, and the boy promptly left. Franklin thought the transaction went off without a hitch. It did not. Nobody noticed.

4:17
"What'll ya have?" The skin and bones that made up an old man gruffly asked.

"Information," was the reply from Jensen.

It was almost twelve hours before the boy would die. The payoff was yet to happen. The transaction was not complete. Nothing had happened but soon would. The air was heavy with a million sins being committed. Light from under doors to the back rooms was the only illumination, other than the lights over the bar. Some sort of music was playing in the background from an unseen source. Jensen didn't care for it, but he wasn't there to listen to music. He jammed a holo-stick into an open receptor port on the bar top. The image of an ornate medallion appeared to hover over the bar.

"What of it?" The old man was a bit evasive.

"Have you seen it?"

The bartender thought and then started to open his mouth.

Jensen gave a stern warning. "Choose your words carefully you old fool; I have a blaster pointed at you under the bar. I will shoot first!"

The wrinkled, old mouth closed. The words it had started to form were lost. Brain waves fired behind his sweaty brow. He gestured to a dark corner with a long, crooked finger before turning his back on the blaster and pretending to wash a glass. The man who had been following Jensen watched and took note.

4:04
Jensen walked down the street. The payoff was yet to happen. The transaction was not complete. The boy was not dead. Jensen had not been to the bar. Nothing had happened but soon would. There was a certain melodic nature to the sound his footfalls made on the metal deck plating that served as a sidewalk. He whirled around, but only the night air was there to greet him. He chastised his shaky nerves and reminded his brain that nobody was following him. In the relative quiet of night, a pursuer would be hard not to hear. The whir of the airships flying overhead was audible,

and it seemed to drift into the background when blended with the noise of late night in the city and the denizens of the dark.

Jensen rounded the corner. His eyes were assaulted by the glow and flicker of neon attached to every wall and roof of every building in the next two blocks. The neon was beckoning as it advertised the darkest pleasures and the worst holo-bars. His spine bristled as he chose a location. This wasn't exactly where he wanted to be, but this was where he needed to be. He chose a door and entered. The man following him watched and took note.

4:25
The payoff was yet to happen. The transaction was not complete. The boy was not dead. Nothing had happened but soon would. Jensen was already in the bar and had already asked for information. When he reached the dark recesses of the room he found a large, semicircle booth occupied by a small wiry kid who looked to be about fourteen, although he was older. The boy was snorting something up his nose. Whatever it was had an effect, and he flung his head back into the burnt-orange, faux leather that upholstered the high back of the seat. His feet went up on the table. Jensen slid in next to him and noticed that he was clad only in an odd green jumpsuit; there were no shoes on his dirty feet.

An impish grin crossed the boy's face. "Your blaster won't be necessary; I'll tell you what you want to know about your father's medallion."

Used to having the upper hand, Jensen felt a cold chill come over him. How did this young child know he was looking for his father's medallion? The boy motioned him closer and whispered in his ear; he then kissed Jensen lightly on the cheek. The boy was not dead, yet. The man who had been following them watched and took note.

4:34
Back out on the street, Jensen's journey continued. He moved uptown where the walks were covered in a squishy, colored, plastic material. This was a welcome relief after walking so many blocks on the hard, metal deck plates. Holo-trees sprung up at exactly nine foot intervals. Their wide leafy tops provided much needed shade from the large red sun that dominated the daytime sky. Thankfully, the holo-barkers that ushered shoppers into the fancy boutiques that lined the street were deactivated at closing time.

Just on the other side of the posh shopping district, Jensen reached his destination. It was a nondescript all night café. He went inside, ordered some coffee, and waited. The man who had been following him watched and took note.

15:26
Jensen nudged the boy's lifeless form with his boot. The moxie was gone from the boy's body, and the child appeared youthful and angelic. Jensen plucked a dart from the boy's neck and remembered what the boy had whispered in his ear. The man watched and took note.

16:14
Franklin's assistant was no match for Jensen; he pushed past her and barged into the office. He tossed the dart onto the massive oak desk.
"I know. All of it."
Franklin was furious. The loose ends were to have been handled. The medallion was to be his. How could this happen? Something went wrong.
"You won't leave here alive," Frankin warned.
Jensen just smiled. The ends were unraveling and nobody could stop what was to happen next. The man watched but noticed very little.

15:27
Jensen reached into the boy's pocket and retrieved the medallion. The man watched and noticed, but it was too late to warn Frankin.

15:12
The boy's bare, dirty feet glided across the polished marble floor of the hallway in Franklin's building. The medallion he had lifted from the large man's pocket was now in his. The theft was unseen; nobody noticed.

16:16
As Jensen died on the floor, he smiled. The medallion was hidden, safe. Franklin would never find it. The man watched but chose not to notice.

the poet

the poet existed
he was in the corner
he was as cold
as the cinderblock walls
that were his jail

the room filled up
he explained the
metaphor was—
and, it was
soon he was alone

he didn't write
he didn't scribble
verse had left his
head
he was dead

A Modern Hero

He heard the screams; they were deafening in his ears. His super hearing was a gift, but also a curse. He must change out of his suit and tie and into his tights and cape. Reporter Mark Dent must become Stupendousman. He must remember to use these names—even in his thoughts—so that copyright lawyers from a large comic book publisher don't object to this parody. Where to change?

The screams became louder; Dent raced around the streets looking for an elusive phone booth. He peered down streets as he passed; he looked in store fronts and down alleys. Nothing!

The woman was on top of a skyscraper being dangled by his arch-nemesis. The screaming crescendoed. A phone booth was imperative! The sounds of her pleading for help echoed in his brain. He pulled out his cell phone to search for a phone booth. Is there an app for that?

Maniacal laughter from his foe drowned out all other noises. Alert! Three new photos have been posted on SocialBook; people are Chirping. About what? The dangling woman, of course. "Hurry Mark, hurry," was rattling around in his head. He had to get there now!

The phone asked Mark Dent to enable GPS to search for a phone booth; he touched "ok" on the screen. Police cars raced by.

Where is a phone booth?

He could hear a bullhorn as a stereotypical Irish-accented police sergeant tried to "talk the man down." He had to get there. The phone's search for a phone booth was interrupted by another alert. Three major news networks were now broadcasting live. SNN was interrupting regular programming with a graphic and scary music. "Crisis in the City" the graphic proclaimed. He really needed to find a phone booth.

The president was giving a speech on three channels now. Reporters were peppering him with questions about the police procedures.

"Are the police handing this correctly?"

"Do we need tougher laws on super villains who are apt to dangle people from roof tops?"

Dent needed to find a phone booth. Where had they all gone? He lowered his glasses and covertly engaged his X-Ray vision. Walls disappeared; furniture fell away. The interior of the city revealed itself. Still, no phone booth! Maybe he should just go home and change. Maybe he should just go back to his office to change. Wasn't there a phone booth in the lobby of the Empire State Building? The governor's S.W.A.T. team arrived. Several red beams dotted the body of his foe. Dent saw this on YouVideo.

His phone jingled in his pocket. Had it found a phone booth? No, it was a text message from his friend and fellow superhero Duce Payne, the Catman.

"Watching on TV. Where are you?"

Dent replied, "Looking for a phone booth. Can you look on the Cat-puter?"

Payne replied with "k."

The screams from the top of the building intensified. The villainous rogue had lowered his victim a bit more. Her voice was panicked. Dent wished for normal hearing; this was hurting his ears. A stupendous headache would be coming on soon.

Our hero was still scanning the urban jungle for the one thing he needed: the elusive phone booth. This was more to keep his mind busy as he was waiting for the response from Catman.

Catman's text would be a relief. The sound of thirteen news helicopters annoyed Dent. Each had at least three cameras trained on the scene, pumping HD video to millions of viewers who were now glued to hour two of "Crisis in the City." Most of them were Chirping. "#whereisStupendousman." There was now a full-blown conspiracy theory about the whereabouts of Stupendousman circulating. Dent could hear the conspiracy chatter from a radio sitting in the window of a building eight blocks away.

Where is a phone booth?

The text announced its presence as the Catman theme played. "Not a clue where to find phone booth."

Even the mighty Cat-puter had failed. Sound was echoing in the urban canyon. Maniacal laugh. Desperate scream.

Just then an idea fought its way through the noise and confusion. Dent remembered. The world headquarters of Gigantic Bell was just a few miles away. There was always a bank of phone booths in front of that place. The quest has begun; the journey started. Dent fidgeted with his collar. The lady screamed; the arch-nemesis laughed. The sounds echoed. The helicopters hummed. The reporters droned on. Dent stepped deliberately, making sure not to run at super-sonic speed. After all, Mark Dent didn't run at super-sonic speed.

"Hurry Mark, hurry," rattled around in his head.

He had to get there now!

Hour three of "Crisis in the City" started with much fanfare and several impressive graphics. Experts had been hastily assembled to talk about the situation. Dent was walking. He didn't know about the latest Chirps and posts on SocialBook. His phone battery was dying. That was the least of his concerns. The voices from the lady, the foe, the reporters, the pundits, and now the crowds filled his head. Dent wanted to turn it all off. "Hang on Mark, hang on," still rattled around in his head. He had to get there now!

The headquarters of Gigantic Bell was a magnificent monstrosity constructed with steel and glass. Just looking at the building seemed to give one the feeling that only impersonal interpersonal communication would transpire within. The Gigantic Bell logo adorned the top of the building. At night it illuminated the area with soft blue light. Mark Dent arrived. He looked for the phone booths. The voices crescendoed in his head. All that remained was the small area at the front of the building that had been scarred by the removal of the booths. Dent wanted to cry. Instead, he slowly walked home. S.W.A.T took out the foe; they didn't even let him explain his master plan prior to doing so. The news coverage ended; the social media feeds fell silent. The helicopters were parked. The president played golf. Mark Dent, reporter, finally took off his suit and tie. He put on a nice, floppy hat and went fishing.

Curtis Becker

A Real Love Poem

The incessant wailing
of the alarm
a plane of frozen tundra
my feet want to retreat
back to the warm cocoon

Morning
Ugh!
Coffee!
Where?

I must jump start my brain
So much depends upon

synapses fire
neural networks form
information flows a path
more paths
they criss
cross

I need to remember to go—

The "whatever it was" in the back of my refrigerator went bad.
Gross!

Is my appointment at 3:15 or—

Our bodies were tangled
as the air
of the summer night
hung heavy
sweat lubricated and became sticky at the same time
our bodies were now—

Curtis Becker
Wait!

Was I supposed to stop at the store?
For cheese?

Your appointment is at 3:15; I think.

Brain overloaded
Reset

Back to you, and us, as one

Smothered by Words

Johnny was one of my best friends until he smothered me in words. It started the day I visited him in the hospital after he had a heart attack. He shook my hand vigorously and told me how much I meant to him. It was probably a side effect of some of the drugs they had him on. Unfortunately, this behavior didn't stop. When I visited him at home, he put his arm around me and gave me one of those side "bro" hugs. It was awkward, especially because he told me I was a wonderful man while he hugged. At church, he was full-on weird with a full-on hug; he told me that he loved me. I bristled and pulled away. This was getting hard to deal with. I avoided Johnny for several weeks, but this just led him to cross more lines with his inappropriate conduct. He called me on the phone to tell me he was thinking about our friendship and that he was sad that he hadn't seen me much. He reiterated how much I meant to him.

It was after this phone call that I decided to let my wife, Cindy, know about this weird behavior from Johnny. Something must have happened in the hospital. Was he still on those drugs? Was there some kind of complication that messed with his brain? Cindy was good at friendships and being social; she would know what to do. Unfortunately, she didn't see anything wrong with what Johnny was doing. She suggested inviting him and his wife over for a cookout. Before all of this craziness, I would have jumped at the chance. I told Cindy that I would rather eat a sandwich. She must have thought I was serious about wanting the sandwich because she left a loaf of bread on the counter with a plate and a knife. She must have gone out with some of her friends because I didn't see her until late that evening.

The next day, Johnny called me while I was at work. This was odd, but at least he didn't get into all of that mushy stuff. Thank God! Maybe he was feeling better. He mainly wanted to know if I was feeling better. He seemed to think that Cindy told him and his wife that I had been sick the night before. I honestly don't know what happened to him at the hospital, but it must have affected his hearing, as well. Johnny tried to visit me that evening with some kind of casserole. My mouth watered for some of his wife's cooking, but I couldn't chance opening the door. I sat on the floor of the bathroom until he went away. I really don't know why I have to be the only one holding it together. Cindy went out with her friends more often, and I ate more sandwiches. I wished I had some friends to grill with. Why did Johnny have to go and ruin everything with words?

The smothering continued. Over the next six months Johnny was relentless. He tried calls, visits, and social media. He couldn't stop with the crazy talk about how he loved me and cared about me. This transitioned into messages with the words "concern," "worry," and "pray" in them. Cindy eventually stopped buying bread, and I had to go grocery shopping. It was here that I ran into my parish priest.

He was browsing in the canned soup aisle when I said, "hi."

Fr. Franklin was so happy to see me. He shook my hand and then put his other on my elbow as if to draw me nearer. He started talking to me about my wife and friends and brought up the words "concern," "worry," and "pray" again. I guess being a celibate causes priests to have no clue about relationships; however, I listened to him out of respect. I smiled in the right spots and thanked him when he was done. I bought a couple of loaves of bread so that I wouldn't have to go back there for quite some time.

After my visit with Fr. Franklin, Cindy changed. I don't know why, but she became distant. When she did talk to me, it was to pick a fight. I guessed one of her girlfriends had really made her upset. I just wished she wouldn't take her bad mood out on me. By Christmas, Cindy was staying with her parents. On the bright side, Johnny had stopped bothering me. His last attempt was at the post office. I was leaving with a package under my arm when he walked in. He tried the priest-like shake and arm hold, but I was cautious. The minute that he went for an embrace, I wiggled out. He professed all manner of awkward things as I was leaving; I was so embarrassed.

I died alone that New Year's Eve. It was a heart attack; I had no wife or friends to call 9-1-1. How could the people who were supposed to care about me let me down? How did Johnny get so lucky while I died?

Cause of Death: Smothered by Words

The Overlord of Ice and Snow

HIS reign of terror
controlling
arbitrary
punitive
cruel

The land, an apocalyptic
wasteland
cold
frozen
devoid of life

A congressman
slides down a hill
A life snuffed out
by a minion tree's icy grip
at the overlord's whim

The masses huddle
cold, icy wind
Then, darkness yields
gray sky

The congressman lives on
he sings on
every
day
to his wife
"I Got You Babe"

The handlers keep the crowd at bay
A proclamation?
Prognostication?
Not yet. He toys with them; lives in the balance

Curtis Becker

Gray skies yield
The sun—HIS source of power
 steals a glance
of the spectacle below
Maybe the sun will retreat

No! It's too late!
HIS speech is low, muffled, terrifying
The handlers nod
The sun hides its brilliance
But not before the deed is done

The proclamation is read.
The subjects have been sentenced.
The sun has been banished.
For six more weeks; HIS reign is absolute

The Overlord!
Groundhog!

He Watched and Took Note

The Domain of Bob's Sack 'N Save

The ball-capped head disappeared around the end of the aisle.

"Crap! This isn't going well," Lucas, the manager trainee, thought. This was the kid who just slipped a ribeye up his shirt! Lucas wanted to impress Bob, the owner.

He rounded the same corner only to see his quarry skillfully navigate around a browsing grandma and her shopping cart. Lucas continued to pursue the lanky kid in the black hoodie. Unfortunately, he ran into a bottleneck as Granny was joined by Mom with two little brats begging for something. Grandma appeared annoyed as she tried to read boxes of bran flakes. The screams from the brats were nearing crescendos as they spotted and were dragged away from the boxes full of marshmallow bits, fruit-flavored pieces, and other things that were part of a balanced breakfast.

Lucas retreated and dashed back down the baking aisle. He loved the smell in this aisle. It was actually his second favorite grocery aisle, behind the coffee aisle. Both smelled heavenly.

He exited the aisle back by the meat counter. His prey was nowhere in sight, but Tommy in the white, blood-stained apron pointed Lucas in the right direction. By the time the deli counter was in sight, he saw his baggy-panted opponent. If he was stealthy, he could make the capture by the bakery. Lucas ducked behind the camouflage of a rack of fresh bread. The sign touted that the bread would be fresh at 5:00 or free. "It certainly does smell fresh," he thought.

Lucas was waiting for the current bane of his existence to come around the rack. The wait seem endless, but the payoff would be huge. Bob was going to be so proud. Lucas could see his own grotesque reflection in the highly polished floor. It was like a fun house mirror, in a way; the white tiles were dotted with tiles of random shades of pastel blue, purple, peach, and banana. He looked in the reflection and saw a proud man stare back. He was strong and confident in his tie and slacks. He just knew he was going to make his mom proud as the best manager trainee Bob's Sack 'N Save had ever seen. Just then, the floor revealed a shadow coming around the rack. Lucas automatically tackled.

• • •

Curtis Becker

The chair Bob had placed him in was uncomfortable; Lucas fidgeted. He looked out of the one-way window at the floor of the upstairs office; his gaze was directed down on the labyrinth that was his domain. From this vantage point he could see all of the grandmas, and moms, and brats, and other characters as they moved about in their carefully orchestrated performance: grocery shopping.

Lucas thought about the inner office, Bob's office. He thought about the view from Bob's window. He had seen it once when he was hired, and it was pretty amazing. Bob was on the phone in the middle of a heated conversation; Lucas tried not to overhear. He looked back out to the maze of shelves and displays below him. The overturned bread rack had already been righted. The floor had been mopped soon after. No one would ever know the chaos that took place there just minutes ago.

Unfortunately, Bob was going to have some bruises after being tackled by his over enthusiastic trainee. The prey and the ribeye slipped quietly out the door in all of the commotion.

• • •

James put the mop away. He grumbled about having to clean up after the latest idiot trainee. He dumped the bucket and rinsed it out. He danced around the stock room with grace as if all of his movements were choreographed and perfectly timed. James delivered the damaged loaves of bread to Gina at the claims desk. "Got a present for you, darling," he said. He gave her his famous smile, and she turned a bit red. This exchange had taken place thousands of times since James first walked in the doors ten years ago. He was a bright, young, handsome high school kid who wanted to make enough money to put gas in his car. A decade later he was a slacker who just wanted to play video games all night. James pushed an abandoned stock cart out of his way with his foot as he simultaneously grabbed two boxes off the shelf. He hopped over a box of trash and danced around a footstool that had been left in the way. This was his domain.

James went on about his duties for another hour. He stocked some shelves, carried out some bags for customers and smiled at everyone. As he was bringing in some shopping carts from the lot, he saw that Bob was showing Lucas the door. He smiled inwardly. He loved to see these trainees fail in his domain.

The Relationship Cycle

It happens every day;
careful to avoid the fray

Don't step in the way,
of Cupid's aim today

Infatuation, Flirting, Courtship

Hard work is about to pay
off—when you get your way

Commitment, Love

Today is Valentine's Day?
Outside grow the flowers of May.

Breakup, Hate

Those feelings need to stay
completely packed away!

This was the display:
my second period class today

It's Time

Frankie decided it was time to leave. She just announced it as a matter-of-fact statement one day.

I asked her, "Why?"

She stated that it was just time and went about packing. I knew the answer to my question. It was time for me to finally take that job. The money would be better. The life would be better. She just didn't want to say anything; it was much less pressure.

She had been packing for days and marked each box carefully with an intricate system involving tape, colored paper, and black Sharpie markers. I think she had five or six markers in all. There was one stuck in her pants, one stuck in her shirt, and one stuck in her hair. Her hair was a bit of a mess in comparison to the neatly stacked rows of boxes that began to populate our apartment. I didn't even hazard to lay anything down for fear that it would be packed away. Daily, I returned from work to find that the items I used every day had disappeared to the far-off land of "packed away" items. The pamphlets about Utah and Salt Lake City started showing up in the mail. At first one at a time, but later they came like an avalanche. By the time that the avalanche arrived, everything was packed away.

The people at work gave me a going away party. They asked about the new job I had lined up in Utah. Several of them jokingly stated that they would be out to visit and ski. It would be quite surreal if any of these people showed up on my doorstep. I didn't say anything. I just laughed and ate another piece of cake. I knew they wouldn't visit. Soon, they would bond with the "new me," the person who would soon sit in my chair and do all of the things that I did. I smiled politely as each person shook my hand and told me how lucky "those people" in Utah were. One of the cleaning ladies wished me luck on my new life in Seattle as she brushed past me toward the door. I just smiled and thanked her.

My parents were not nearly as "thrilled" as my co-workers had been. They used words like "mistake" and "tragedy." My mom cried. My dad lamented. Frankie promised that we would stay in touch and that they were always welcome to visit. My mom cried more. My dad lamented more. I touted the advantages of the digital age and offered to install Skype on their computer. My mom cried even more. My dad lamented even more.

• • •

It was late afternoon, and we were way behind schedule. Frankie and I were filled with anticipation as we passed through the suburban sprawl. Chicago saw the taillights of our moving van as the landscape began to trade development for trees and grass. The side of the interstate was green. Cars passed us as we could only seem to muster 55 miles per hour in the ancient machine we had inherited from the moving gods. We cheered as we crossed the Mississippi River. It was dark and we were the only ones who heard it. Frankie had been asleep, and I had nudged her into the conscious world just in time for the celebration. She was back to dreamland before we cleared St. Louis. We ate breakfast in Kansas City.

I was asleep when the trees disappeared and woke up to the brown harsh landscape of the high plains of western Kansas. We had dinner east of Denver in a busy restaurant that was fed by the interstate. As planned, we stayed for several days in Colorado with Frankie's half-sister. I couldn't wait to get back on the road; it was time.

Our lumbering vehicle became even slower heading up into the mountains. I was glad the interstate had a really slow lane. It was populated by semi-trucks, RV's, and people like us, crawling our possessions up the side of a mountain at 40 miles per hour. Frankie slept as we crawled through the high country. She missed Berthoud Pass and Rabbit Ears Pass. She missed the white knuckle decent into Steamboat Springs and only stirred slightly as Highway 40 inched toward Utah. I drove through the night; it was time to get to our new home. When she awoke, Frankie spotted the skyline of our new city and smiled.

•••

Frankie and I settled into a house in an older neighborhood. It was a rental and not nearly as posh as the apartment in Chicago had been. Not that the Chicago place was fancy, but this place was hideous. In fact, it was a refugee from the 70's. The shag carpet and Z-brick around the fireplace may have been someone's dream at one time. The décor was not ours. Frankie hated the house. She also was not fond of the neighborhood, the weather, or the people. She found fault with everything. She soon was using words like "mistake" and "tragedy." She cried and lamented.

My new co-workers were nice. Occasionally, they asked about my former life, but it was polite conversation to kill time. Only Frankie cared about Chicago. We talked about the old apartment, the old neighborhood, the weather, and the people. Mom and dad called more and more as we soured on our new life. They were now using words like "opportunity" and "fresh start" to describe a move back home. One day Frankie said it was time. Mom used words like "ecstatic." Dad started organizing the Utah rescue mission. The boxes were packed in a hurry this time. I hadn't been at work long enough to be asked to participate in the social ritual of "going away."

We picked up dad at the airport. He had hired a moving van and supervised the loading of all of our worldly goods. I sat in the corner feeling like a failure. This trip was much easier. I slept all the way to Midway airport. It was good to be home, even if I was a failure.

In our new apartment in Chicago, Frankie said it was time. It was time for me to get over feeling like a failure and to embrace this life. Pamphlets for self-help started showing up in the mailbox. At first one at a time, but later they came like an avalanche. I went to a meeting or two, but I couldn't get over my setback. I knew it was time. I left Chicago bound for a place from which I could never return. My mom cried. My dad lamented. Frankie was devastated.

the process i can't control

my hands are possessed
i have no control
they scribble
they peck at the keyboard

my hands are possessed
they serve another master
they scribble and peck
i am along for the glorious ride

i watch as the Creation unfolds
i hope this Poem is worth printing

Curtis Becker

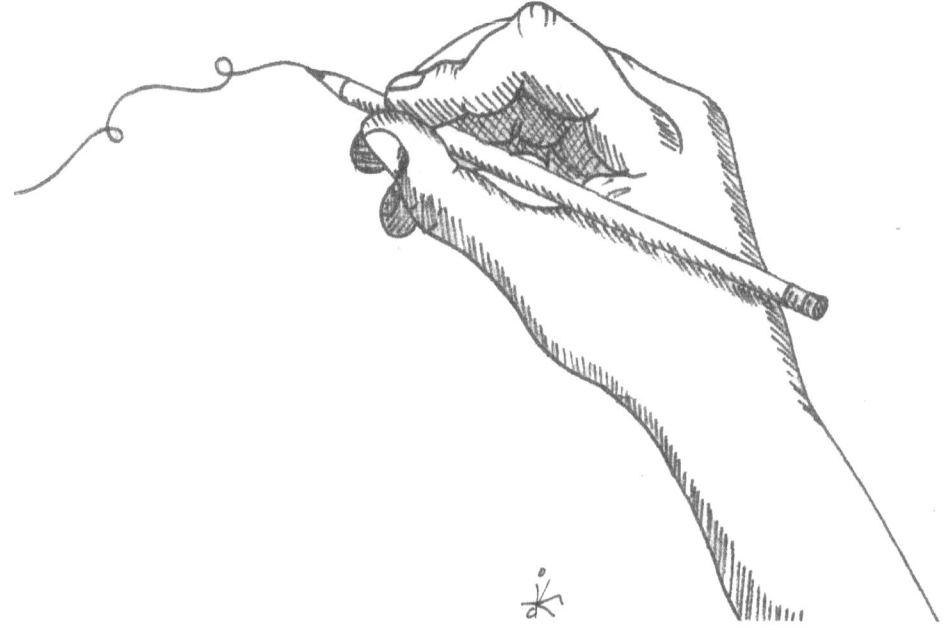

Forgiveness

I wish I could be with my family today. To celebrate my Mom and Dad. The congregation knows Mr. and Mrs. John Swift, the happiest couple in the church. They have been together for forty years, and I wish this gathering was for that reason, for them. This morning they occupy a pew at the front. This is out of the ordinary; normally they sit at the back and hold hands, but today is a different day. They are here for me, and I am sorry that it has to be this way. Dad always dresses up for church, but today he is in his best suit and a new tie that he was saving for a special occasion. Maybe his anniversary? Mom is in a dress that belongs at Christmas or Easter services. They look knowingly at each other and smile. They are happy to be together, but sad at the same time. Dad sighs with contentment as he grabs Mom's hand. At least that gives him some comfort. The church smells of the amazing array of flowers gathered up at the front; it also smells of old wood and burning candles. Mom smiles at Dads touch. His rough callused palms rub against her dainty soft hands; her skin is soft and fragrant like the flowers. His is worn and rough like the wood in the old rural church we attend.

Mom scans the pews around them. Today they are surrounded by all the kids and grandkids that they don't get to see as much as they want. Finally, everyone in church at the same time; Mom will be happy about that. My eldest sister Jenny with her husband Rob is in the church. Their five kids are sitting quietly next to them like a perfect row of stair steps. Right behind them is my brother Jimmy, the next oldest. He doesn't have a family; he is unmarried. Jimmy is sitting with his nieces, twins Jessica and Chloe. Next to the Twins is their father, our brother, Freddy. Freddy's wife Cathy is not able to be in the church because of a "work thing." Mom is a little disgusted by her absence, but will never say anything. I bet she wondered if Cathy realized how important this day was; Cathy did know, but couldn't bring herself to face the day. It was a reminder of what happened to her best friend years ago. Somehow, I know mom did wonder about Cathy's absence and thought some less than Christian things about her motivation. I forgive Cathy for not being at the church and Mom for what she is thinking. Jessica waves at her grandmother. Mom breaks her somber church face and smiles and waves back at Jessica. She is like a kid when she was with her grandkids. She pokes Dad in the ribs; he turns around and waves at Jessica, too. My wife, Mandy is seated next to Mom. Mom releases Dad's hand and grabs Mandy's. She pats the top of it. Our kids are seated next to Dad. He uses the opportunity of his free hand to sneak some small books and toys to the three young boys. He places his finger over his lips as if to say, don't tell Mom or Grandma. The boys winked at Grandpa to let him know that the secret was safe with them. Typical Dad. I forgive him for teaching the boys his ornery ways. They don't quite understand what happened, yet. I'm thankful that Dad, Jimmy, Freddy, and Rob will all be there to help them come to terms with this and to raise them. They will need these guys in their lives without me.

Dad is happy to see his siblings, my aunts and uncles with their kids and grandkids seated behind his family. It is great to see everyone. He thinks about the meal they will all share in the church hall after services. He knows the food might not be great, but the fellowship will be amazing. My Uncle Steve catches him looking back and smiles. Dad nods his head to show that he appreciates his entire family's support. I forgive Uncle Steve for the falling out with Dad that drove a wedge between factions of the extended family. Hopefully, dad will forgive Steve, and Steve will forgive Dad. The family will be whole once again.

Gladys Johnson is a regular member of the congregation, a fixture in one of the front pews. Today, she was glad to give up her seat so that my family could be up front. She and her late husband played cards with Mom and Dad on a regular basis; she is quite fond of her friends and wanted to be in the church today. I remember how much she smoked. Then she would douse herself in strong perfume to cover the smell. What she created was a smell of stale, musty, lavender. Gladys thinks back to her first days in the church when Mom had immediately befriended her and her husband and helped them feel welcome in a new place. She remembers all of us kids sitting with Mom and Dad every Sunday morning. Jenny was always so tall. She was also prim and proper and would help her mother keep the others in check. Jimmy and Freddy were close in age, but nothing alike. Jimmy was a little mischievous boy. He was the one most likely to be the subject of Mom or Jenny's ire because he was turned around sticking his tongue out or making funny noises as the preacher tried to talk. It wasn't that he was a bad kid; in fact, he was a favorite in the church. He was just a little mischievous at times, kind of ornery like Dad. Freddy was the opposite of his brother. He was quiet and brooding. He was never any problem in church, but always a worry for Mom and Dad the rest of the time. He never seemed happy growing up. Thankfully, he left that phase behind as he entered adulthood. As Gladys remembers me, a tear forms in the corner of her eye. It is wiped away with one graceful stroke of her tissue. I am/was the youngest and I could be found on Jenny's lap during church; she always took care of me. People said I was the cutest kid because I was always smiling and waving. People also said that I would grow up to make something of myself. Unfortunately, I didn't really get a chance.

Today, I wish I were with my family. I wish I could be there with Mom and Dad. I wish I could be there with my brothers and sisters. I wish I could be there with my wife and kids. I wish that Mom and Dad were celebrating their fortieth anniversary. But they are not, and I can't be there. I don't think they will hold it against me; I am dead. My cold and lifeless body lies in the coffin at the front of the church; however, that isn't me. The lid is closed to spare everyone the horrific damage that has been done to my face. It didn't hurt; I was already dead by the time my face skidded across the pavement. I know I should have worn a helmet; I hope they can forgive me. It is a small blessing that everyone didn't have to see my face. Unfortunately, Mandy and Dad looked when they claimed my body. Mom couldn't bring herself to go in. She feels bad that she didn't. I wish she knew I didn't want any of them to see it. There is no need for forgiveness.

As the minister begins speaking, the faces of the family begin to show pain and anguish. Many openly weep and cry. Members of the congregation cry, as well. Tissues work overtime. The minister tells the story of me, the young boy who Gladys Johnson remembers. He tells of my journey through his teenage years and of the friends that will miss me. He talks about my survival of several tours of duty overseas and the loving wife and family who eagerly awaited my return. He talks about the motorcycle accident that claimed my life and of the truck driver who hit me. He asks that the congregation pray for this man who may never be able to come to terms with what he did, the young life he snuffed out. My family prays. The congregation prays. I already forgave him.

Modern Sonnet #13

I literally don't know
what to say about her—
her face is like a million rays
of sun and I want to write

a Shakespearean Sonnet.
But I don't want to rhyme
or count the beats in the
line

Her hair was Hollywood gold, or was it auburn
and the gold made the metaphor work?
Is she the face that sold a million songs online
or is that her character in this poem?

Boom, crash, bang
reality comes for a visit

She bought some makeup at the drug store the other day.
"Do you need concealer?"
Yeah, I asked.

I think I will live in this poem while she is mad.
Rhyming Couplet?

The Starlight Motor Lodge

The man was nice to the lady at the front desk. He was more than nice; he attempted to brighten her day with his pleasant banter and easing chuckle. Maybe she would overlook the paltry sum of money he presented and give him a nice room after all. The lady handed him the "key." It was one of those "new" card keys. He had used one once but wasn't fond of them. Not that he had occasion to check into a hotel much. Actually, this was more of a motel he thought. He would make the best of whatever was behind the door; all that mattered was that the boy was coming.

The flight of stairs was hard on his knees, but he tried to smile and be pleasant as he climbed them. He gave a nod to those descending. His small, blue Samsonite case clung to his side as he entered a long, dim hall. The stale smell of cigarettes, booze, and sex filled the hall. This wasn't the impression he wanted to make when meeting the boy, but what could he do now? It was happening, and this was a place that could facilitate the meeting.

The man reached the end of the hall, room 219. He inserted the "key" and nothing happened. He turned it over and spun it around, but still nothing. He went fast. He went slow, but still nothing. Darn! Now he was going to have to return to the front desk. He was perspiring now, and not wanting to wreak his church clothes, he considered leaving the Samsonite and his tweed jacket at the door. He looked at the stained carpet beneath his feet and the wallpaper peeling from the wall beside the door marked 219. A quick decision was made; it might be best to take them with him. He straightened his tie and adjusted his collar before turning to make the trek back down the hall with the yellowed walls and floral wallpaper. The boy would not be impressed.

As he walked, his mind wandered. What was he doing here? It was all the fault of the Internet, the computer his nephew had helped him set up. Before that, he didn't even know what a website with personals was or that you could set up something like this using it. Before this quest, the man didn't know that he could use his new cell phone to text people and confirm a place and time like this.

The man's last text had been, "in room 219 at the Starlight Motor Lodge on Hwy 27."

The response had been, "K."

Curtis Becker

Who responds with one letter? He had taken $100 from the cookie jar at home and slipped out the back door without being noticed. The adventure began! He would return the missing money to his mother as soon as he could.

The woman at the front desk felt bad. She accompanied him back to 219. This trip included a ride in the service elevator; he was grateful for that. Once inside the room, he was disappointed. The smell was better than the hall, but still stale. The bed was tired; it slouched from years of bodies. The bedspread appeared to be stained. With what? He didn't want to venture a guess. Cobwebs hid in the corners as dust clung to a rather large vent in the ceiling. The bathroom fan was present but hanging from the wall by a couple of wires. His nervous inspection was done. This was, after all, a place that something like this could be done; it couldn't be done with his mother around. He just wished he could make a better impression. A chair in the corner looked new. He set down in it after turning on the TV.

His phone danced and sang.

A message from him. "Running l8."

The man had learned that the letter "l" followed by the number "8" was texting speak for "late." He was getting good at this. His response was "ok," even though his brain was tempted to use just the "K." He recalled the initial conversation that they had via text messages. Zach had sent him a picture right away. The man went to it and stared at the boy's dark features. He felt like he had known this kid forever. He hadn't. The picture made him nervous at first. Zach wasn't wearing a shirt in it, and he felt like he was downloading "kiddie porn." He told the boy this.

The response was matter-of-fact. "Im 19 & was @ lake."

It's like solving a puzzle every time. The response didn't make him feel better; most of the boy's texts were this way. They made him uneasy.

He tried to get comfortable in the chair. It was the nicest thing in the room. He propped his feet on the Samsonite and tried to relax. The TV droned on about some nonsense. He got bored and opened the door to people watch. A young girl with a baby was moving into the room next to his. She looked scared. He smiled at her, but did not say anything. He didn't want to seem too creepy. Someone down the hall was opening and shutting a door. Outside a large truck was stopping in the street. Its air brakes gave their customary groan as they stopped the motion of the beast.

He Watched and Took Note

Where was that kid?

His phone danced and sang.

"Gotta sneak out."

That made him uneasy.

"Might be tough."

Was he not coming?

That possibility hit him like a sharp winter wind. It sent shivers down his spine. As if on cue, the heater vent in the corner coughed and sputtered to indicate it was trying. The room was cold, but the possibility of no meeting was even colder.

"What is wrong with me?"

He tried to clear his mind by watching TV. He adjusted the volume; he wanted to hear it without disturbing the baby on the other side of the paper-thin walls. He took a blanket from the bed and draped it over his body. That was better. He drifted into an uneasy sleep.

When he awoke, he found two hours had disappeared. The phone had not danced or sung. The reality was sinking in. The boy was not coming.

"What is wrong with me?" the man thought.

He composed a message to the boy. It was full of emotion and basically told him to go to hell. He erased that and composed another. This was in Zach's own matter-of-fact style.

"Not coming? I am leaving. Sorry it didn't work out."

The phone danced and sang.

"Wait! I told you I had to sneak out. It might be late."

Three TV shows passed by his eyes. He had some coffee at the diner next door. The service elevator took him back up to his floor. The lady at the desk had never stipulated that his ride was a one-time thing. The girl next door was out in the hall smoking a cigarette. He smiled again. Thankfully, she wasn't in the room smoking around the baby.

His phone danced and sang.

"Come get me?"

The man was nervous; he dropped the phone. The girl with the cigarette picked it up and handed it to him.

"Here," she said as she smiled at him.

He mumbled "thanks" as he turned around to head for his car.

"Where do you live?" was his response on the phone.

The boy gave directions to a corner in town, and the man gave the boy

Curtis Becker

a quick description of his car. When he arrived at the corner, a tall, skinny, dark-hooded figure jumped in his front seat.

"Zach?"

"Yes."

They drove in silence for several blocks, then an awkward conversation of plesentries ensued. This was followed by more silence. At The Starlight Motor Lodge on Highway 27, they climbed the stairs; he didn't want Zach to think he was old, so the frieght elevator wasn't mentioned. The girl in the hall smiled at them as she lit another cigarette. Once inside the privacy of the room, he made his move. He grabbed the boy and pulled him close. Zach did not struggle. They embraced. He kissed Zach on the cheek. The boy was warm; he pulled him closer. He couldn't believe this was happening. For the first time in nineteen years, he was holding his first born against his body. He wept. They wept.

He Watched and Took Note

I'm Not Kevin Rabas

I'm Not Kevin Rabas.
he has cool facial hair
and a snare for rhythm.
I forgot to shave this morning,
and left my trombone at home.

I'm not Kevin Rabas
He brings Lisa,
a talented singer/songwriter
I come by myself
Some of Lisa's CD's are in my car.

I'm not Kevin Rabas
People pay money
to take his classes;
Children risk truancy
to avoid some of mine

I'm not Kevin Rabas
It's like turning on the TV
And Johnny Carson has the night off
And I'm Jay Leno
Or Joan Rivers!

I'm not Kevin Rabas
Kevin is the Poet Laureate of Kansas
(if you didn't know)
I published a poem a few months ago
And called my mom

Curtis Becker

If you came tonight to see Kevin Rabas,
Sorry! I know how you feel.
I came to see Kevin, too
The silver lining is this
Tonight, you are on next!

When I substitute as host for Kevin (Kansas Poet Laureate, 2017-2019) at his monthly open mic, First Friday at Ellen Plumb's City Bookstore, I lead with this poem.

Frank Won't Back Down

As he dreamt, Frank the gambler was sitting in an old wooden chair in an empty room. He clutched his cards to his chest as smoke from an unseen source rose to the celling and the large orange lights beat down on the table. He attempted to play the Ace of Hearts. "Wrong suit!" someone yelled. As he stroked his beard, the room melted away, and a desert was revealed. The large orange sun made him miserable. His hands shook as he tried to play a card. The alarm sounded. The dream soothed his fears. "Shuffle up and deal."

Writing Love Poems with Kevin

I was writing love poems with Kevin
Because it was almost Valentine's Day
And Marcia asked us to

Five dollars and vintage keys struck paper
Love spilled on the page like marvelous metaphors
The client's heart was a simile that only we could write

I told my students that I had to hurry
After school; I couldn't stay
I was writing love poems for five dollars, for Valentine's Day

Oh, gross, said they
You are writing love poems
And you are so old

I'm writing love poems with Kevin and
He's around my age
And he has some printed in books

That's different, said they
He's really cool
And you're our teacher

Acknowledgments

While writing these acknowledgments, I am overwhelmed with gratitude and want to thank every person in the known universe; however, this course of action isn't practical. For over thirty years, I have been writing creatively and have been blessed with wonderful teachers, mentors, friends, family, and colleagues. Without all of you, this book would not have been possible.

As the dedication in this book indicates, I owe a lot to my parents. I wish my dad were here to see this achievement, but we lost him twelve years ago. To my mom, **Toni Cummings**, thank you for reading to my siblings and me when we were young and for taking us to the Goodland Public Library when we started reading on our own. You fostered an atmosphere of inquiry and creativity. I remember how you painstakingly drew and cut out paper action figures to go along with a fantasy world of which I longed to be a part. Thank you for being my first writing teacher, my first proofreader, and my biggest champion.

Marcia Lawrence, thank you for sharing your knowledge and supporting me with spectacular advice as I started Kellogg Press and published this book. Thank you for Ellen Plumb's City Bookstore. It is a treasure in Emporia that celebrates authors and artists and gives us a space to share our work. I value you as a friend and mentor. You are as fiercely independent as Ellen herself, and for that, we should all be thankful.

Kevin Rabas, your plate is overflowing, and yet you make time to be a champion and advocate for so many of us in the writing community. Thank you for your encouragement. When I met you, I believed that the author part of my soul had been left behind somewhere; you reminded me that it is always with me. One is a writer when he writes. You have been a friend to me and my students and many great pieces have been written because of your influence. Kansas couldn't ask for a better Poet Laureate.

Mary Jane Ryals, as my first, formal creative writing teacher, you gave me the power to master words and taught me how to make a story ebb and flow as I married description with action. Sentences and paragraphs that previously plodded through a plot line became music that effortlessly lifted the reader toward the climax. I value the advice you gave about being an author, a student, and a person. Thank you!

John Somer, you wanted to understand the world and our relationship to it. As an undergraduate, I took every class you taught because the facination with figuring this out was mine, too. Along the way, I learned that all words mean something and that the best stories evoke emotion. We all have a different perspective on the world, and good storytellers find a way to speak to everyone. Some of my pieces have a bit of Kurt Vonnegut's world view in them; I discovered him because of you. A weekend was spent devouring *Slaughterhouse Five* because references to it popped up in your lectures regularly. Since then, it has been my favorite novel. Thank you!

Mike Graves, you are a dedicated and brilliant writer who wrote two of my favorite novels. I value your friendship and appreciate your kindness. Thank you for reading my manuscript and for the coffee and conversation. Your observations and advice strengthened the final product.

Hazel Hart, you are an amazing editor. You found inconsistencies that most would have overlooked. You asked questions that elicited rewrites and gave suggestions that made change palatable. Thank you for the detailed reading of my manuscript; this book is better because of your efforts.

Cheryl Unruh and **Tracy Million Simmons**, as strong voices in the writing community, you bring others together. Your workshop gave me the ability to find community as I shared my writing for the first time in years. Thank you. Each of you is an exceptionally talented writer and a great mentor who encourages everyone to be better.

Austin Anderson, thank you for driving down from Manhattan to be on the cover of this book. You sat in alleys and stood in crumbling doorways as we found the perfect shot. While many people know you as the face of Bramlage Coliseum and the K-State Wildcats, I hope that some will recognize you as the "Watcher."

Dave Leiker, you are a talented man behind the camera. My vision became real through your lens. Thank you for scouting every 'seedy' place Emporia has to offer as you looked for the perfect location. Your photo captured the perfect scene.

Kari Ludes, you have an amazing talent for the visual arts. My vision became real through your hand. Thank you for the masterful drawings that give this book the 'classically illustrated' feel I wanted.

Joe and Rita Buchanan, thank you for tackling the initial draft of my manuscript. It needed your thorough reading.

Thank you to the **Emporia Writers Group** for welcoming me with open arms and helping me to find fellow wordsmiths.

About the Author

Curtis Becker, a distinguished teacher embarking upon his twelfth year in the classroom, has inspired students at the middle school, high school, and college levels. Becker holds professional, highly-qualified credentials in both Kansas and Colorado. When not working with his students, he focuses on his own writing. Most recently, one of Becker's pieces appeared in the anthology, *Bards Against Hunger: 5th Anniversary Edition*. This book, *He Watched and Took Note* is his first. Becker is also the owner of Curtis Becker Books and its imprint, Kellogg Press. He offers writing, editing, design, and publishing services.

Becker calls the beautiful Black and Gold District in the heart of Emporia, Kansas, home. Here, he participates in and supports the thriving downtown community. Becker was born and raised in Goodland, Kansas, and lived for over a decade in the Yuma, Colorado, area. He earned a bachelor's degree in English from Emporia State University and a master's degree in fiction writing from Southern New Hampshire University. As an undergraduate, Becker helped to create ESU's literary magazine, *Flint Hills Review*, and served on the editorial board for the inaugural edition. He is a member of the Kansas Authors Club and the Emporia Writers Group.

www.ingramcontent.com/pod-product-compliance
Lightning Source LLC
Chambersburg PA
CBHW032049290426
44110CB00012B/1013